Dog and Man

The Science of Potty Training

An Essential Manual for Every Dog Owner

DEDICATION

For all the dog owners out there looking for the answers to potty training and other dog training mysteries, this book is for you.

Table of Contents

INTRODUCTION

Important things to know before you start reading.

I have written this book to be informative, entertaining, and groundbreaking.

Grammar may suffer a bit, but you will get the flavor of how I speak and teach, that has proven to be very effective.

To make things move quickly, I refer to all dogs as he.

The title *Dog and Man* refers to canines and humankind.

Dog means canine. Man means humankind.

At times, when you are reading this book, my words may seem a bit harsh.

You may think I don't love dogs in a mushy, heart-is-melting way.

Well, I do love them.

I work with and train dogs every day and have for 30 years.

I talk to them, pet them and enjoy being with them.

I Love Dogs!!!

No matter how passionate I get about dog training, my intention is to teach you what is real, and make this process clear and effective for you and your dog.

In my opinion, dogs are the best animal companions for humans in the world, hands down!!!

When we touch our dogs, we experience a positive, rejuvenating, calming, healing event.

Having a dog can lower your blood pressure, slow down your heart rate and help you live a longer, healthier, life!

It's just the miracle they perform for us and it's a wonderful arrangement,

Dog and Man.

So What Is *The Science of Potty Training*

Imagine saying a word to your dog, at the moment you decide, at the place of your choosing and he goes potty.

Imagine your dog never going in-your-house, on-your-carpet, in the spot behind-the-chair, in-the-den, again.

Imagine being absolutely clear on what you need to do in every potty training situation.

That's *The Science of Potty Training!*

For decades dog training has been approached as if it were a mystery.

It is, in fact, Science.

As you read on, you will find yourself saying, "Ah, now that makes sense! I never thought of it that way, but, it makes perfect sense!".

This method is made up of specific, easy to understand solutions to specific problems, based on your dog's evolved, inborn, behavioral predispositions and the appropriate behavioral modifiers.

You do something simple to change or fix the way your dog was born and naturally acts.

This book will educate, prepare and guide you to potty train your dog, by yourself. And keep it working for the rest of your dog's life, and every dog's life that you own, for the rest of your life.

I've written this book in sections and a particular sequence to best prepare you for potty training.

You will have the greatest potty training success if you read it all in that order and don't jump ahead.

Read the stories. Look at some of the mistakes other people have made, so you don't make those same mistakes.

Take it all in.

So, here we go!

Foundation

The foundation on which this method is built

The way your dog's brain and body work

And

What you need to know before you start potty training

Understanding Your Dog

There's a lot of misinformation out there about dogs and sometimes we are persuaded to believe urban legends, myths and outright lies.

I want to help you recognize what is real and true.

To learn what your dog is and is not.

I want to teach you what works and what does not work.

Let's start with how Human Nature distorts our perception of dogs.

It's not our fault, but, our frame of reference is purely human.

A wise man once said,

"We don't see things as they are . . . we see things as we are."

He meant we see everything as human!

When we see our dogs as human we may treat them wrongly.

These first few sections will help you see your dog for what he is, canine.

It is so important that you read them thoroughly before you start potty training to get the best result!

My Furry Child?

The important differences between your dog and human children.

As surprising as it may be, sometimes the my-dog-is-a-human-child misconception puts our dogs in danger and even hurts them.

> For example, chocolate, citrus, avocado, grapes, raisins and onions are superfoods for your child.

> Yet, all of these may kill your dog!

Your baby cries when he's hungry and you need to feed him when he does.

> If you feed your dog every time he whimpers,
> he will likely become morbidly obese.

Your child can follow complex instructions,

> "Go upstairs, put on your pajamas, brush your teeth, choose a book and wait in your room."

Your dog can only respond to simple, grunt like commands,

> "Fido Bed!"

So, if you are talking about your dog and you say,
"Well, he's just like a two year old child...." Stop for a moment and think.
A dog is nothing like a human child: physically, cerebrally, or behaviorally.

Although you must feed your dog, house and protect your dog, take him to the Veterinarian, and care for your dog in a way that seems similar to caring for a human child, the similarities end there. Interacting with your dog, in full acknowledgement of that fact, will give your dog what your dog really needs.

I know you want to do what is best for him and that's exactly why you are reading this book. You also want to make your life, as a dog owner, as pleasant as possible. That's why you want to potty train your dog.

The great news is you can do both!!!

So, keep reminding yourself: "He's a dog!"

Reactive Not Reasoning

Why punishment doesn't work
And
How the dog brain does work

Many dog owners are convinced that punishment is the way to go and that it really works.

It isn't and it doesn't!

Why doesn't it?

Because dogs can't process punishment.

Punishment is a complex concept and experience that requires a thinking, human brain.

Imagine someone saying to their tail chasing, not recognizing himself in the mirror dog:

"You peed on my genuine, two thousand dollar, Persian rug, Fido. That was Bad! Now you are going to have Time Out in your crate, think about what you did and no treats for you!!!"

Some of you have been told, influenced and led to believe this is what you should do.

But, the canine brain is far too simple to process that complex information.

"Why can't my dog process punishment?" you ask.

Because he is Reactive Not Reasoning.

Here's why this is so confusing:

The human brain is infinitely complex and we see dogs as human.

The dog brain is very simple but we believe they are complex thinkers.

In reality:

Dogs can only react to their body or their environment:

Doorbell rings - dog barks.

5

You say, "Wanna go for a W-A-L-K?" and dog gets excited.

Dog feels full bladder - dog pees.

No plan.

No spiteful intent to pee in your house.

Bladder full = dog pees.

Dogs are not human or human like at all and you should feel glad about that.

If your dog thought like a human and had human emotions and behaved like a human, you wouldn't want him!

When you left for work, your dog would think about it and complain that you left him alone all day.

He would feel many human emotions and say he was sad, bored, cry tears and become depressed.

Your dog would argue with you and get angry at you.

And when you came home, sometimes, he would not be happy to see you at all!

But, thank God, he doesn't think like a human.

Thank God he does not have human emotions.

He does have his own kind of canine compulsions, that make him always look happy to see you when you get home.

His own kind of canine compulsions that make that tail wag every time you talk to him.

He has his own reactive brain that makes him your Man's Best Friend.

He is *Reactive Not Reasoning.*

Caught In The Act

What to do when you catch your dog going potty in your house.

Since I can't tell you everything in a few pages, and you need to know some stuff right now, here is the first thing.

If you catch your dog in the act:

> Do not yell.
>
> Do not shake a can of pennies.
>
> Do not hit your dog.
>
> Do not rub his nose in "it".
>
> Do not react, at all!

If you do something negative, like the list of don'ts above, your dog will develop a negative association with peeing or pooping in your presence.

Your dog's brain will observe that:

I pee in the presence of my owner and he yells at me
or
hits me
or
I hear a loud, scary sound.

Your dog experiences that going potty near you equals negative.

That will make your dog avoid going potty when you are present.

Because he wants to avoid the negative, you may have to walk and walk and walk some more, before he finally pees or poops.

If your dog is *Caught In The Act*, do nothing, say nothing, just read on.

Puppy Love

You can train puppies and dogs of any age.

Some of you reading this book have puppies that you just brought home.

Some have young adults and others older dogs.

Good news . . . . The age of your dog has little or nothing to do with potty training.

The canine brain works the same way at five weeks, five months, five years and all throughout your dog's life.

The sooner you train him, the easier and better your life and his life will be.

As to the physical challenges: Some puppies, aged birth to eleven weeks or so, can have a tough time controlling their bowels & bladder, when compared to an older dog.

This means you can't afford to vary from the instructions in this book, as your puppy can't hold it.

Most experts define a puppy to be not older than 22 months of age.

There are some changes to your dog's body and behavior specific to young puppies growing up and older dogs breaking down.

But, we can train them all!

So, puppy owners, be of good spirit.

Jim Dandy To The Rescue!

You can train your rescue dog, no matter what!

Many of you out there have rescued your pup and wonder if he can be potty trained.

You wonder why your dog was surrendered or abandoned at the shelter, and if that "why" will prevent successful potty training.

Did something bad happen to him?

Was he abused?

I have heard these questions and concerns hundreds of times.

These are normal and common thoughts.

So why was my dog abandoned at the shelter you ask?

And the answer IS….

Most often, dogs are what they are and always were.

Your dog's behavior, most likely, never was the product of abuse or bad experiences.

Rather it was his behavioral predisposition the day he was born and the reason he was abandoned.

It is nature not nurture.

And that's probably why someone gave up on your dog.

Many rescue pups take a lot of work and some owners, due to their life circumstances, just can't or are not willing to do that work.

The good news is you can succeed where the previous owners failed, and with some tender loving care, potty train your rescue pup!!!

Second Time Around

You can re-train pee pad-trained and litter-box-trained dogs

Some of you have already pee pad-trained or litter-box-trained your dogs, and now want to convert them to regular, go-outside and do-your-business-in-the-backyard training.

You may be worried that the old training will interfere with the new training.

It won't.

You can always teach old dogs new tricks, as long as that old dog is healthy.

Don't worry, we will get your dog re-trained to go potty outside, regardless of what he has already been trained to do.

Just use the method, like everyone else, and ignore the fact that you have used the other.

This potty training system will work for you, even if your dog is used to going in a litter box, on pee pads or on any other material.

The critical element here is that you crate your dog during the brief potty training process and do not allow access to a litter box, pee pads or other material. That means the crate is empty and there are no pee pads or litter box inside the crate.

The Rules

Why your dog needs rules.

Your puppy's evolved brain is compelled to search for the dog rules, the rules of social harmony and survival.

Once he finds those rules, he is compelled to follow them, as finding and following the rules is ingrained in your puppy's evolved brain.

He is looking for those rules from the first moment he is born and again from the first instant you are with him.

The earlier he finds the rules, meaning the earlier he is trained to fit into your life, the earlier your dog can relax and follow those rules.

"Why?" you say.

Well, as dogs went through the cruel, heartless process of evolution, that I call, "The Crucible of Death", those who found the rules and followed them, survived.

Dogs who failed to find and follow the rules of survival, exposed themselves to danger, died off and their genes died with them.

Dogs with the compulsion to find and follow the rules, survived and passed that trait on to your dog.

Finding the rules and following those rules is a deep-rooted, overwhelming, powerful compulsion and an innate part of your dog.

Create the rules.

Be The Rules!

The Chain Of Success

Why you must go step by step, and how skipping steps is bad.

I can't tell you how many times people have asked me,

"I wonder what would happen if…?"

And after the "if" comes a way of skipping a step in the training process and testing the training before it's completed!

They want to see "if" the training will fail when we do their test. Maybe because they want just-add-water-instant-dog-training and to avoid the work and time training requires.

It might go something like this,

I wonder what would happen if… "instead of carrying the puppy outside, we just put him on the floor on the way outside?"

You can easily imagine what will happen.

The dog will pee or poop in their house.

Pee or poop is now all over their floor.

Bad idea.

It's just common sense, uncommon in today's world, that testing training before you are absolutely sure it's rock solid, set in the dog's brain, is a bad idea.

Don't do it!!!

Training is always accomplished in a chain of success, one single link at a time.

This requires patience, discipline and precise execution.

And it's worth it!

Be Realistic

A story about Bella

And

Why you need reasonable expectations

Because dogs aren't perfect.

This is a sad, somewhat tragic story, about an owner who just could not or would not be realistic about owning a dog. He must have expected a robot that looked like a dog. But, he never should have bought a living, breathing, real dog.

Hopefully, you will gain perspective on how unreasonable and out of touch we humans can be, sometimes, with our man's best friend.

And now for our story:

A client came in and hired me to board and train his German Shepherd puppy. She was a beautiful female named Bella, but she had some . . . . problems. So, this man, we'll call him Joe, told me that potty training was very, very, VERY important!

When people say this it usually means they can't stand dog pee, poop, smell or any change in their house that the dog brings and it's an omen of bad things to come.

Well, after getting a life-threatening health problem under control, one that Joe totally missed, and keeping Bella an extra week at no cost to Joe, we were able to save her life and get her potty trained.

It was really tuff though, because Bella couldn't control her body at first.

After suffering all the trials and tribulations at our training facility, when Bella went home, she had only one accident in her crate.

Only one accident!

That's great!

You might be thrilled with that, right?

Well, that wasn't good enough for old Mr. Joe. He decided that even though sweet little Bella was obedience trained to perfection, would heel, sit, lie down and come when called, (I can hear you out there saying, "I want my dog to do that!")
and was finally potty trained, that just wasn't good enough.

Old Joe was determined to find fault with Bella. So he called us and said Bella "smelled" and he just couldn't tolerate the "dog smell".

Wow, a dog that smells like a dog.

Who could have seen that surprise coming?

That is one of those "you-have-got-to-be-pulling-my-leg excuses."

Of course, dogs have a bit of a smell.

They're dogs!

So, Joe dropped sweet little Bella off, and abandoned her at the animal shelter.

Wow.

The moral of this story is:

Be realistic.

Horseshoes and Hand Grenades

The importance of precise execution of dog training and handling.

Almost is good enough in horseshoes and hand grenades, but, not in potty training or any dog training.

Dog training is a specific, rifle-shot endeavor.

You have to hit the bullseye every time!

Do it just the way this book teaches and you will hit that bullseye.

The research and development has been done for you.

It's been proven that it all works thousands and thousands of times.

Follow the procedure and it will work for you!

It Is What It Is

The difference between Dog and Man.

Potty training your dog will go much better when you truly see the difference between Dog and Man, when you perceive and handle your dog, as a dog and not as a human being. Accepting and working within this context is vital.

Your dog, and every dog, is much Dog-Happier:

When you treat him the way he instinctively wants and needs to be treated.

When you treat your dog consistent with the way Evolution made your dog.

Why is this so hard for us to do? Because humans and dogs are opposites in many ways.

> Dogs: Seek out and are comfortable in very small, tight, dark, enclosed spaces or "Dens". Under your bed, in your closet, under a footstool, etc.

So, dogs love their crates.

> > Human Beings: Are claustrophobic, get creeped out in elevators, closets and crawl spaces.
> >
> > Some humans even have panic attacks in elevators, tight spaces and crowds! So, humans say;
> > "I would never want to be in a crate!"

Dogs: Can only react with either their evolved reaction or with a conditioned reaction, as the result of operant conditioning or training.

So, sometimes they do things we don't understand and don't seem logical to us.

> > Human Beings: Reason. We take in all the available information, process it, think it through, compare it to past experiences and then formulate a decision.

Humans combine instinct, intellect, emotion and memory to arrive at a complex decision.

No matter what we feel, want to believe or what we think we see, the above statements are true and part of why we love our dogs.

Canine is Canine.

Human is Human.

And never the twain shall meet.

It Is What It Is.

A dog.

The Den

Denning instinct, behavior and its origin

Nature's Crate

And

Why your dog is comfortable in his crate

When I am doing an orientation session with a dog training client, the first step in our thirty-day Board and Train Program, one of the family members often goes into convulsions when I bring up crate training.

They muster up all the misinformation they have stored in that head, all the myths, misconceptions and outright lies they have heard and try to tell me that crate training is cruel or wrong. It is neither.

Dogs developed a powerful, natural denning instinct, through millions of years of evolution and the process went like this:

First, dogs who stayed out in the open were easy prey, killed off by predators and did not reproduce!

Their genes were eliminated from the gene pool.

Dogs who used Nature's crate, the den, randomly crawled into very small caves, holes, hollowed out trees or piles of rocks with only one opening.

These completely enclosed spaces, allowed them to attack anything that came in that one and only opening. Snakes, spiders, predators and humans could not easily attack or harm evolving dogs in such a small, tight den.

The den, Nature's crate, was their safety, their comfort, the key to short term survival and long term evolution.

They survived and did reproduce!!!

Those denning dogs became the big fish in that gene pool.

Your dog comes from that big fish.

"But my dog is a domestic dog," you say.

18

Well, domestic dogs are insignificantly modified versions of evolved, wild dogs.

Think about it. How many dogs have you seen in domestication go under the Ottoman, under a break in the front porch, under an end table, under a bed or any other spot that is small, dark and confining?

Sometimes they go in of their own free will and can't get back out!

Denning, using Nature's crate, is what dogs have evolved to do!

This is what your dog is compelled to do!!!

So, using a crate is the right and best thing for successful potty training.

Potty Training Health Issues

Lazy-Good-For-Nothin' Dog?

A story about Dozer
And
How a serious health problem can look like bad potty training behavior.

I remember this sweet, gentle, cute, loving Bloodhound puppy named "Dozer". He was extremely small for his breed and age.

Kind of pathetic looking, and you couldn't help but love him.

Dozer's small size was definitely a clue that there may be something physically wrong.

Note:
> When a dog is a different size from average dogs of the same age and breed, it may be an indication of physical defects or illness.

It actually made me sad to see how weak this poor puppy was.

Dozer's owner, Moe, brought him in for training and told us Dozer was "lazy" and on a "three week hunger strike."

Wow!!!

You have to be kidding me!!!!

Dogs are purely evolved, reactive animals.
If they're not eating, it's because their brain is telling them not to.

It's because something is wrong!

Something is wrong with the dog, the dog's food or the environment.

The owner here was making the classic, ginormous mistake of giving his dog the uniquely human ability to think.

He was causing his innocent, sick little puppy to suffer needlessly!

Dozer was so weak he could barely move, even with considerable coaxing. He just couldn't do things like a normal, healthy puppy, and we had to figure out why!

So, I went with Dozer to the Vet and sure enough, he was full of worms and had a serious respiratory infection.

He was so full of worms that he had no energy.

He didn't even have enough energy to eat!

The worms were literally consuming his food, suppressing his breathing and sucking the very life out of him!

So sad.

Moe was convinced his sick little puppy was lazy and stubborn and just refused to eat or learn!

Moe's my-dog-is-human-and-thinking fantasies almost killed Dozer. This misconception is much more common than you may realize.

In reality, dogs cannot think like humans.

Remember: eats own poop, allows you to control him, chases tail, etc., etc., etc.

They have a binary, reactive brain and process information in a simple manner.

This makes them loyal and willing to give their lives for us!

This is why they are Man's Best Friend.

So read on carefully, with your irreplaceable, precious pup always in mind.

He's counting on you!

Back to our Dozer story…

Sweet, little Dozer was physically sick, weak and barely alive.

Since he was a dog, and dogs can't talk, (except in movies), he couldn't explain that to his owner.

All Dozer could do was be a dog, a very sick dog.

His brain was telling him to do what dogs who lived millions of years before had done, be still, in order to survive.

During evolution, this random reaction to sickness resulted in a higher rate of survival in recovering dogs and became Dozer's evolved behavior.

And now for our happy ending!

We got rid of Dozer's worms, treated his infection and he got much, much better.

Then we trained Dozer from the starting point of a healthy dog, with great success!

And Dozer and Moe lived happily ever after!!

I want all your dog's stories to have a happy ending.

So, read this next section carefully, and learn how to detect if your dog is sick and needs Vet care.

That may fix the problem making him go potty in your house and it's the right thing to do.

Tip of the hat to all the Vet's out there!

The Answer Lies In The Question

Questions and answers to determine if your dog is sick,
making potty training difficult.

Note:

This section is not the complete guide to diagnosing your dog. Rather, it is a tool, intended to make you aware of indicators that tell you he may be sick.

Because, sickness can and does affect potty training, getting a baseline health exam to determine what is "normal" for your dog is an excellent idea. This will be an invaluable reference for your Veterinarian when your dog gets sick.

You should have or find a Veterinarian who can examine your pup regularly and help you keep him in tip top shape!

Q: Does your dog have worms?

Puppy owners listen up! Puppies nearly always have worms. The question is, how much? They have either recently been wormed and only have a small amount, or they are full of worms and badly in need of worming.

After the initial 11 weeks of life, worm your puppy on a regular schedule, about once every four to six weeks, and things will go more smoothly.

Be aware that monthly heart wormers, although an excellent resource, may not kill all the worms and parasites your dog can acquire.

Adult dog owners: your dog also needs to be on a regular worming schedule, about once every four to six weeks.

Consult your Veterinarian for the appropriate wormer and schedule.

Q: Does your dog have a stomach virus?

A stomach virus will absolutely make it impossible for your dog to control his bowels. Intestinal viruses usually produce bad smelling vomit or feces.

Take your dog to the vet if:

Your dog has diarrhea or vomiting,

Your dog suddenly has smelly poop or foul breath,

Your dog emits a rotting fish odor,

Your dog suddenly has a bad gas smell and you have not recently changed his food.

It's easy to make a joke about bad smells and miss a deadly serious illness.

In puppies, these symptoms can be life threatening!

Q: Does your dog have a fever?

You can check with a rectal thermometer.

Now, that really shows you care!

If you are familiar with the way your dog's ears usually feel on the inside, you will recognize the difference when your dog has a fever. A healthy dog's temperature varies from 99 to 102.5 degrees. It's a great idea to take your dog's temperature several times while he is healthy, to get a "normal" or baseline temperature. With that important piece of information, you can easily spot a fever when you suspect he is sick. This will also be a valuable piece of information for your Vet.

Q: Does your dog have a churning stomach or runny stool?

Changing foods can completely turn your dog's insides upside down.

A churning stomach means soft or runny stool and no potty training!

This usually happens when you go from a food with high protein and low fiber, to a new food with lower protein and higher fiber.

So, if you switch foods, go to an equal or higher protein food and the stool will get firmer.

The makes for much easier clean up!

Q: Was your dog potty trained and then suddenly began to pee or poop in your house?

Uh Oh….

Dogs don't suddenly get un-potty trained.

There's always a reason.

Something in their world or their body changes and their potty training breaks down.

If your dog was potty trained and suddenly begins to go in your house it could be:

> Sickness,
>
> A new animal or person in your home, or stuff happening outside your home,
>
> A serious health problem, like a tumor on the bowel or bladder.

So, be careful to look at what is happening around your dog and consider what might be happening inside your dog.

If your dog gets un-potty trained after you have finished this book, return to the crate training procedure.

If the problem goes away it was behavioral.

If the problem persists, it is physical and your puppy needs to see his doggie doctor.

Home On The Range

How free feeding and overfeeding can interfere with potty training

Dogs who eat too much food, have too much food inside them and will poop more frequently. This is a serious problem for potty training.

But, many people believe free feeding is good.

I have had countless dog owners come into my kennel and proudly tell me that they leave food out for their dog.

They say, "He just grazes all day long."

"He knows how much he needs."

They tell me this, thinking they're doing something good for their pup. Acting with the very best intentions.

Here are the facts:

Through evolution, dogs who ate at every opportunity, tended to survive.

Those opportunities were rare and dogs who did not eat at each and every opportunity died off.

Most domestic dogs will eat many, many times more food than they actually "need".

Through evolution this served them well.

Today, living in our suburban homes and left to their own devices, dogs may eat so much food that it can destroy their health.

We have to take control and rescue our dogs from this overwhelming, evolved compulsion.

One For Good Measure

The solution to over feeding
And
Getting your dog to a healthy weight by measuring his food.

Always measure your dog's food, with a standard measuring cup, and watch your dog eat all of that food.

Only feed your dog the amount that is necessary to keep him lean and fit.

With most dogs of most breeds, the outline of his last two ribs should be visible when he twists or turns to the side.

If your dog has a long thick coat of fur, rub his side. You should be able to feel each rib & the space between, but under a little padding.

Keep in mind, you should not be able to see your dog's ribs when he is standing straight.

Rest assured, this is normal, correct and healthy.

Also realize that most dogs you see or know are likely overweight and the owners believe their dog's obese state is normal.

So be prepared to hear; "Your dog is so skinny!"

Keeping your dog lean is absolutely essential to providing a high quality of life for your man's best friend. He will avoid potential health problems and injuries, run faster, jump higher, have more energy & chase a ball longer when he is trim, taut, terrific!

That fit condition makes it much easier for him to be potty trained.

If your dog is overweight, do not follow the recommended feeding amount on the bag of dog food, as it is only a suggestion!

A large dog, ninety to one hundred pounds, can be quite healthy eating one and a half to four measured cups of premium food per day. But, every dog is different, and you need to figure out the precise amount that's right for your dog.

I have seen crazy metabolism scenarios play out many times.

Some dogs, even very small dogs, can eat five or six measured cups per day and be slim and trim, depending on how many calories they burn.

You need to write the book on your dog, when it comes to how much he eats and how much your dog weighs.

Your dog should always be slim and trim, with a taut tummy that scoops up to a narrow waist.

All dogs, of all ages can and should look like this.

When your dog is very young, from birth to one year old or so, he should always be gaining a small amount of weight. At the same time, he should be very fit.

Between one year and three years of age, dogs finish growing.

(Kind of surprising, but, yes they grow until around age three.)

So, feed just enough and keep your dog trim, taut and terrific.

Remember, your dog cannot restrain himself!

So, you have to!!!

If your dog is obese, initially reduce the quantity of food by 25% until your dog trims down to a tight waist as described above. Then go up (if too ribby) or down (if still overweight) one quarter cup at a time until your dog's weight stabilizes.

If you want real world proof, watch Animal Planet . . . .

Not one obese lion, tiger, gazelle, zebra, or dingo . . . .

Your dog was born to be trim, taut, terrific!

It will make your potty training work better!

Take control and do what is right for your dog!

The Straight Poop

The digestive process of dogs.

In order to know how quickly after eating and how often you need to take your dog out to go potty, you need to know that your dog's digestive system and your digestive system are completely different!

Dogs can eat raw meat. We really can't get away with that.
Please, don't read that and start feeding your dog raw meat.
That could make you and your dog very sick.

You: Digest food in 24 to 72 hours from beginning to end.
No pun intended. That's as much as three whole days!

You can take your time when you need a potty break.

Your dog: Digests his food in 2-10 hours, or less!

That's less than one half of one day.

This means you can't expect your dog to "hold it" for very long.

It also means that when you put food in your dog, food is going to come right out! Because the digested food is waiting to come out as the new food goes into the digestive tract.

Often times, after you feed your dog, he will be ready to poop in less than five minutes.

Food in - poop out.

Their digestive cycle is very short and always happening.
He's making more every second of every day.

Think of it like a Play-Doh machine.
While you're putting the clay in the front end, it's just about to come out the back.

Feeding your dog and emptying your dog out are one continuous operation.

So, during the potty training process, your job is to put the new food in and be ready to empty the old food out in 5 to 15 minutes.

Doggy Day Timer

Timing versus the need for a fixed schedule.

Dogerella

And

Dogs can't tell time

People always state with absolute certainty Dog Training Myth Number 412:

"You have to put your dog on a schedule!

Sssssskedule Sssssskedule Sssssskedule!!!!

He needs to be on a schedule!!!!

Well, doesn't he?"
Simply put, NO!

You need to be logical about when food goes in your dog and when it is likely to come out.

That's timing.

You need to have a manner in which you consistently conduct potty training, feeding, watering and handling your dog.

For some people, a schedule fits their life.

6:00 a.m.: Take dog out
6:10 a.m.:   Bring dog back in
6:15 a.m.: Feed dog
6:30 a.m.: Take dog out again

For these people, a schedule is perfect.

To these people: use a schedule.

For others, a daily schedule is just not possible.

That's Ok.

To those people: relax, don't worry. Use the same potty training, feeding, watering and handling system I am teaching you in this book, at the times that are possible for you. Get the timing of the operation down and you and your dog will be just fine.

Absent some cue, signal or trigger that tells your dog it's time to go potty, your dog won't spontaneously pee or poop at a scheduled time, like some maniacal, horror movie pooping alarm clock.

A lot of people believe dogs can tell time. I remember a friend of mine, who had way too many dogs and he absolutely believed his dogs could tell time.

Every night, at 12:00 a.m., he would shuffle his butt around on his couch, put on his shoes, jangle his keys, pick up the leashes and wha-da-ya-know?! His dogs would magically get super excited at the stroke of midnight, like Dogerella.

Gonnnnnggg!!!!

He would proudly announce in an excited voice, "See! They can tell time!!!"

As if Prince Charming had arrived out front with a giant pumpkin carriage and a pooper scooper.

And I told him over and over:

"You're right Bill. It has nothing to do with your we're-going-for-a-walk pregame-show."

Shuffle your butt.

Put on your shoes.

Jangle your keys.

Pick up the leashes.

And voila!!!

Your Cinderelladogs know it's midnight."

Now, back to the real world….

Dogs do recognize associated cues such as physical activity, sound, light, vibration, movement, odor, that tell them something is about to happen.

When you are on a schedule, those things simply happen at the same time each day, on-your-schedule.

You are the only one that sees the clock, or is aware of the time.

You do something, or several somethings, that signal your dog he is about to go out.

Dogs don't know what time it is.

Your alarm clock goes off at 6:45 a.m. and your dog recognizes the alarm sound as an indicator, a cue, a signal or a trigger to an association that you will take him out in ten minutes.

That's all it is.

Nothing more.

So, don't worry about the precise time.

The operative word here is system, not schedule.

Screaming In The Wind

Why you can't teach your dog a lesson.

Potty training your dog is a very sane activity.

You never need to do crazy things.

Rather, you do need to be logical because your dog is reactive, not reasoning.

Lots of crazy things are done, in pursuit of potty training dogs.

> Here's an example:

> I remember looking in shock and horror at my friend's dog walking into the room with a shoe taped to his mouth.
> (Yes, a shoe!) I asked my friend, "What's that about?"
> He told me he was, "teaching his dog a lesson."

This is the same thinking that makes people rub their dog's nose in his own poop.

Yuck!!!

You can't teach your dog a lesson.

Dogs don't learn lessons.

Dogs can't learn lessons!

Unlike our complex thinking brain, theirs is a simple reactive brain.

They can only react to stimulus.

Dog is stimulated; dog reacts.

The canine brain has two types of reactions: evolved and conditioned.

Hiding in the closet or bathtub during a thunderstorm is a good example of an evolved reaction.

> Here's how this came to be:

33

During evolution, some evolving dogs hid when they heard thunder off in the distance. Those evolving dogs survived.

Of course, it makes sense that evolving dogs who avoided thunder and thus heavy rain, flooding and lightning, survived more often. They passed on that behavior to their puppies through their genes. The random surviving reaction of avoiding thunder, produced the evolved behavior of domestic dogs hiding in the closet or bathtub during a thunderstorm.

Now let's address conditioned reactions.

READ THIS NEXT LINE VERY CAREFULLY!!!

You can only train your dog to react to a stimulus: a cue, a trigger, a sound, a noise, a grunt, a movement, which signals his brain to do something.

Training is creating conditioned reactions to associated triggers.

You say sit; the reaction is: your dog sits.

This conditioned reaction, like all training, is simple association. Your dog hears the sound sit and he puts his butt on the ground. Sit = butt on the ground. It's always that simple.

Hot fire = move away. Thunder = hide in closet. Sit = butt on ground.

Trying to "teach" your dog a complex "lesson" is like Screaming In The Wind. This would require your dog to possess the ability to process language and to reason. He can't.

You may expend a great deal of energy, as you yell

"Stop blowing my hat off Wind!!!"

at the top-of-your-lungs and feel exhilarated afterwards.

But, the Wind does not understand or respond to your message.

Neither does your dog.

So how do we Potty Train our dogs?

Like this….

34

PREPARATION

How to get your home and your day ready for potty training

What equipment you will need

And

How to manage your dog physically during the process.

The Right Tools For The Job

The necessary equipment for potty training.

Before you start your potty training day, you will need a leash, a collar, a plastic airline kennel, paper towels and enzymatic cleaner.

Get a regular 6 foot leather leash and do not get a retractable leash as it is unsuitable for dog training.

If you have a small to average sized dog you can get all these things online. If you have a dog over 75 pounds you will need the largest airline kennel, a Vari-Kennel 700-Giant. You will probably need to have your pet store order it for you and pick it up there.

So now you have a crate, a leash and collar. These are very important, non-negotiable tools, necessary to potty train your dog.

And now we start your potty training journey, at the beginning of your busy day.

How To Use The Crate and The Leash

No matter what you have been told before or what you believe at this moment, because this is a brand new method, you are starting from scratch.

First, you will need a plastic airline type crate, just big enough for your dog to go in, stand up, turn around and lie down.

When the dog is in the right sized crate, his ears will touch the roof when standing, and body length will take up the entire crate, standing or lying.

Any extra room will give the dog space to pee or poop.

Remember, your evolved canine loves to be in the smallest, tightest space he can cram himself into. He is a denning beast!

Note: Here's a quick trick for later, when you're cleaning your plastic airline crate.

Attach the top of the crate to the bottom with only two or three wing nuts. When you need to clean it, remove the wing nuts, take off the top, door, and clean the bottom. You can even carry the bottom outside.

Why a plastic crate over wire?

Wire crates bend, and dogs often break out, damage your home and hurt themselves in the process.

When your dog has an accident, the removable tray in a metal crate becomes filled with urine. If you try to move or carry a flat tray filled with urine outside, you may spill it in your house or on yourself. Not fun!

I don't want to get nastygrams saying I made you get dog pee on yourself.

So, don't buy a wire crate!

If you have a wire crate it is sooooo worth it to get a plastic airline kennel for potty training. You can find a used plastic airline kennel on social media.

Owners of little puppies, listen up! Start with a small crate and graduate to larger sizes. Graduating up in crate sizes is best, as it leaves no room for accidents.

If you are using a larger crate, block off the extra space with a space divider.

Note:

> If you will be potty training your dog alone, you may want to get two crates.
>
> "Why?" you ask.
>
> Wellllll, sometimes Pookie will have an accident in the crate.
>
> When you have two crates, you take your dog out, let him do his business again and put him in the clean crate.
>
> That way, he will be secure in the clean crate while you clean the dirty crate. Two crates are definitely better than one.
>
> After you finish potty training you can sell the extra crate or give it away.

Next, your dog will have two modes during potty training: in the crate and on the leash.

1) In the crate.

If you are not taking your dog outside keep him in the crate.

If your dog is out of the crate, even for a few seconds, and not on the way outside to go potty, he may pee or poop on your floor.

If you are watching a movie, making your dinner, eating food, talking to someone in person or on the phone or doing anything that requires any part of your attention, keep your dog in the crate!

There is no letting him out to stretch his legs, letting him out to run around, letting him out to...whatever.

During potty training, a short two week period or so, you must follow this rule to have success.

2) On the leash.

This means the leash is attached to your dog's collar, with you holding the leash and focusing your full attention on your dog, every second he is out of the crate.

Every time you take your dog out of the crate, it's a training exercise.

No matter how we perceive it as "free time" or "just relaxing", it is a training exercise to your dog and more specifically to your dog's brain.

Because, every waking moment of consciousness is a training exercise to your dog.

When your dog is out of the crate, ask yourself these questions:

Will I train him or will the environment train him?

The answer must be that you will train your dog.

"Free time" or "just relaxing" means the environment will train him and that's bad.

Ask yourself;

> "Will I pay attention to my dog
>> one hundred percent of the time he is out of the crate?"

To achieve successful potty training, the answer has to be yes!

This bears repeating:

Having your dog On The Leash means that your dog is wearing a collar, attached to a six foot leash, and that leash is in your hand, with your eyes on your dog.

No harnesses!

Only a leash and collar.!!!

The purpose is to be able to control and direct your dog and keep him within your reach every second he is out of the crate. You must be able to gather him up and take him out to go potty as soon as you see the signs.

Don't tie the leash to a chair and forget about your dog.

Don't lay the leash on the floor and forget about your dog.

Don't let your dog walk around dragging that leash and forget about YOUR DOG!!!

Don't put a movie on, fall asleep, and wake up to a steaming hot pile of "I-should-have-stayed-awaaaaaakke!!!" on your floor.

Do keep your eyes on your dog or put him back in the crate!

If your dog goes potty in the house, while you were looking the other way, it's your fault!

He's a dog!

Remember, your dog doesn't think, can't think, won't ever think.

You have to do all the thinking.

That means you can't let your dog down by accidentally "training him" to go potty in your house.

You have to train your dog to go potty outside with consistency.

And remember, you cannot hit him, yell at him, shake a can of pennies or perform any other negative action if he goes potty in your house. As I said before, this will train your dog that going in your presence is bad and he will not go in your presence outside either.

On the other hand, if you leave your dog out of the crate, don't watch him, he pees in your house and observes that the experience goes well, then, to your dog, peeing in your house equals good. Oooops!

Your dog is trained by what he observes.

Don't let these bad observations happen!

Take your dog out and follow the potty training procedure!!!

The Out Of The Crate-On The Leash potty signs are:

* Standing suddenly * Whining * Walking in a circle

* Sniffing the floor * Looking up and sniffing the air

* Turning around and looking at or sniffing his rear end

There may be others that I have left out, but to be clear, watch your dog for anything different in his behavior.

So, you keep your dog on the leash, in your sight, with your eyes on your dog.

Watch for the signs that your dog needs to go potty and follow the potty training procedure.

"You mean I have to have my dog in sight at all times when he's out of the crate?"

Yes!!! At all times!!!

The potty training period is brief.

You can easily endure it and the benefit will last a lifetime.

Food, Water and Behavior In The Crate

Let's talk about In The Crate:

Before you put him in the crate,
make sure you've emptied your dog's bowels and bladder.

Do not put food or water in the crate.

When I say this there are people who go into a panic:

"WHAAAAAAAAATTT?!!!"

"Won't my dog die of starvation?!!"

He'll get totally dehydrated, turn into a ball of dust and
blowww awayyyyyyy!!

"Don't dogs always need **food and water?!?!"**

As to starving, no he won't.

As to constantly needing food and water, no they don't.

You will feed and water your dog out of the crate.

And make sure he has the proper amount of each.

If you leave food in the crate, your dog will get the potty training process out of sequence. He will eat in the crate, you won't notice him eating and he will have to poop when you don't expect it.

If you leave water in the crate, your dog will also get potty training out of sequence.

He will drink the water, have to pee and you won't notice.

He will spill the bowl of water and be wet in his crate.

Once you have put your dog in the crate, watch and listen.

Pay attention!!!

Question: Is he suddenly whining, moving or scratching?

If yes, take your dog out and follow the potty training procedure.

Question: Was your dog lying down and now has stood up for no apparent reason?

If yes, take your dog out and follow the potty training procedure.

Question: Has your dog suddenly started to walk in circles in the crate?

If yes, take your dog out and follow the potty training procedure.

If there is any kind of major change in your dog's behavior in the crate, take your dog out and follow the potty training procedure.

If you are not looking at your dog, you may miss the potty signs.

"So, are you telling me that I have to keep my eyes on my dog all the time during potty training?"

No, but, until your dog goes potty, you need to be very aware of him.

After he goes, you should be good for awhile.

In The Crate or On The Leash with your eyes on your dog!

This is easy to say and hard to do.

But, it's a short, worthwhile process and you can do it!!

Myths Legends and Lies

Urban legends and outright lies that interfere with potty training your dog

Born Freeeeeeee!!!

Why allowing your dog to run free is bad.

Over the last twenty eight years of being a professional dog trainer, I have heard the most hysterical, irrational, dangerous ideas about keeping and handling dogs. Especially, when it comes to crate training versus letting your dog run free. Let's try to put it all in perspective and keep our feet firmly on the ground.

Letting your dog run free, untethered, inside or outside, is a training defeating, reckless idea. It is commonly based on the fantasy that dogs are better off in the wild and somehow need open space in domestication.

Here are some sobering facts:

Fifty percent of dogs born in the wild die before their first birthday.

Every day pet dogs running free get hit by cars, stolen, poisoned,

injured in fights with strange dogs, foxes, coyotes and

can even get out of your yard and disappear from your life forever!

When they are running free in your house, they will poop or pee and you won't see it.

While you are potty training your dog,

you have to totally control your dog's activity and movement.

You can NOT allow your dog to run free

inside or outside your home and successfully potty train your dog.

43

Dogercise

How dogs don't exercise in the wild and why your dog doesn't need to.

When allowed to behave naturally, dogs are sedentary, rarely moving or not moving at all. They do nothing unless stimulated, thus their bodies have evolved to maintain good, physical condition without a great deal of activity.

No Dogercise.

Adult dogs in the wild are only active when seeking food, water or defending themselves and their group. Yet they remain physically fit and strong.

No Dogercise again.

So, taking your dog out to go potty is enough activity.

There is no need or benefit to letting your dog "run around".

No Dogercise.

Only potty training.

How To Potty Train Your Dog

This section is the *How To* of the book: from the beginning of your potty training day, to tucking everybody in at night.

Potty Training Sunrise

How to take your dog out in the morning.

So, you get up in the morning and your dog is in the crate.

Before you start stimulating the stuff you want to end up in your backyard, out of your dog, get dressed quietly and don't talk to your dog.

You may feel it is necessary to say,

"Oh Pookie, I'm so glad to start another wonderful day of Dog-Human companionship with you my little Ookie Dookie!!!"

You may even want to bend down and kiss him on the nose.

MWAAAH!!!"

But it's a bad idea at that moment.

By the way, I kiss my dogs on the nose and make the Mwah sound too.

Just at different times from Potty Training.

Pookie is giving it all he's got to hold his pee and poop in.

The proverbial dam is about to burst. . . .

And when you talk to him and kiss him on the nose you're stimulating it right out of him.

Not fair!

Dogs, early in their potty training and at an early age, are very sensitive and will need to go potty every time they are significantly stimulated.

That means when you get out of bed, when you get home from work, when you are loud or excited, when you are moving around or stand up after being still, etc., it will stimulate your young dog.

You get the idea.

When he is being potty trained, anything the least bit different, the least bit exciting, the least bit stimulating makes your dog need to go potty. Later he will be able to control himself with these stimuli.

So, namaste, be present in the moment, quiet and don't stimulate your dog.

After you are dressed and ready to go directly outside:

Calmly and silently go to your dog's crate.

Open it.

Slip the collar over your dog's head and get to the door fast!

If your dog is small enough, or if you are potty training a puppy, carry him outside in order to prevent the possibility of your dog quickly squatting and peeing or pooping on the way.

You have to make sure you do everything possible to keep the pee and poop in your dog, before he gets outside.

So, if you can, carry your dog outside for a few days and then advance to walking him on the leash.

When you get to the door say, "out", open the door and take the dog outside. You are creating the association that the sound, "out", equals the door opening and your dog going outside.

This little trick may come in handy later.

So, now you have gotten outside, with your dog, and nothing came out inside.

GREAT!

You're on your way!!!

Silence Is Golden

Why you need to be quiet while your dog is going potty.

Next, put your dog on the ground and follow him around very quietly.

Silence is required!

In this case you want your dog to pee or poop without being distracted or stimulated.

You need to be very quiet and very still.

Do not pull, tug or keep tension on the leash, so your dog can concentrate on the business at hand.

The leash should be as loose as possible.

If you talk or move, your dog will react to you and stop going potty.

So, don't chatter your dog to death when he is trying to do something very private.

"Go Potty Go Potty Go Potty Come On Pookie Go Potty
    You Can Doooo It!!!"

Stop!!!

When it comes to Potty Training:

Silence is golden.

You wouldn't want someone outside the bathroom door talking to you while you're sitting on the throne, makin' a doo doo, now would you?

Tap, Tap, Tap "Hey-eeeee…. How's it goin' in there?

Everything comin' out alriiiight?

You don't mind if I open the door now, do you?"

And yes, I realize that I just made a human analogy.

I'm trying to get in your head.

You need to understand this, somehow, even though it's in human terms.

So you don't mess it up for your dog.

Just be quiet and wait.

If you distract your dog, he will not go potty, because his Submission and/or Self Preservation Drives will stop him.

Dogs need to be comfortable by perceiving that they are safe and in Social Harmony with you.

Meaning you allow your dog to move about, without manipulating or dominating him.

So beeeeeeee quiet!!!

Potty On Demand

Marrying the word "empty" to peeing
and
Training your dog to go potty on command.

This section can teach you how to make your dog go potty on command.

You say a word.

Your dog goes potty.

Not only is this a great way to entertain your extended family on Thanksgiving Day, but just think about how handy this little trick can be when you're in a hurry to leave for work, or taking a pit stop from your wild road trip, and on and on....

So, here's how you do it:

> When your dog starts doing his business, as the urine is coming out, and your dog is feeling that urine come out, you are quietly saying, "empty, empty, empty, empty." Say it almost in a whisper, literally as if you are speaking to a hypnotized person whom you don't want to wake.

> By quietly saying empty four times, you are attaching or marrying a word to the feeling of peeing. You repeat the word four times because one time is a freak occurrence, two times is a coincidence, three times is a pattern and the forth one is to make sure your dog heard you at least three times.

> You are creating a conditioned association: the sound "empty" equals peeing.

> Your dog empties his bladder, without being stimulated or dominated, and the word empty is married to the feeling of peeing.

> After about two weeks, you will be able to prompt your dog to "empty" by saying this magic word.

Of course, it's not really a magic word. It's a cue: a sound, a noise, a grunt that causes your dog to respond with a conditioned reaction, namely peeing.

Plainly and simply, "empty" triggers peeing.

You can choose a different word, but I like empty.

This is just one example of how you have to communicate with your dog in a way your dog's brain can process.

Here's a bonus.

If you take your dog out, say empty, and he does not pee, you know he doesn't need to. Mystery solved.

There's No Place Like Home

Why your dog will walk and walk and not go potty

Is much more likely to go in a familiar place

And

Self Preservation

People often tell me they take their dog out to go potty, walk and walk and walk some more, and their dog doesn't go.

They get back to the house and the dog either goes in the garage, the house or the crate.

I have heard this complaint thousands of times.

It may happen to you as you begin potty training and you need to know why it happens now.

"So why do dogs walk and walk and not go potty?" you ask....

Let' exclude the owner yelling at the dog or rubbing his nose in his poop or other previous bad training. For the purpose of this example, the owner performs his part of the potty training procedure perfectly. He comes back from walking the dog and he goes potty in the house.

Some of you out there right now are saying,

"Yes! That happens to me! Why?

The answer this time is…

Self Preservation!!!

Self preserving dogs, like those described in this scenario, are born with the behavioral predisposition to hold it when in an unfamiliar area.

Their evolutionary ancestors who did this, lived to go another day.

By contrast, dogs through evolution who would feel relaxed going potty in an unfamiliar area, were often killed off by predators.

51

Let's face it, when your dog is in the humiliating, awkward, dog-imitates-airplane-landing position, he is surely vulnerable.

Evolution gave your dog the traits he has at this very moment, by way of your dog's ancestors doing things randomly that resulted in their survival.

They didn't "know" what they were doing.

They did things because they were naturally inclined to do those things, and as a result of that natural inclination, they survived.

Their offspring with the same behavioral traits survived and so on and so on and so on.

As each generation passed on this trait, it became more pronounced.

Dog breeding today is often indifferent to the behavior of the dog parents. Two dogs look "pretty", so, the owners breed them. These dog parents may have bad temperament and do things that are undesirable, like holding it until they get home. So, we get self preserving puppies.

It's easier to tolerate this non-pooping, self preserving behavior, if you understand it is instinct.

So, today the unfamiliar area stimulates your dog's Self Preservation Drive, as result of his inborn, natural, behavioral predisposition and your dog doesn't go.

Your dog's brain stops him from doing things that would have made his ancestors vulnerable to attack and killed them.

When your dog gets home, to the familiar area, where no threats are perceived, he feels comfortable and away it goes.

There's No Place Like Home!

So, what do I do when my dog goes for a walk and won't go potty?

Rebound, my friend, rebound!

Rebounding

What to do if you take your dog out and he does not go potty.

Rebounding is absolutely one of the most significant tools ever devised to potty train your dog.

And, once again, it is time to rely on our old friend, the crate.

When you get back, after your dog has not gone potty, your dog needs to go directly in the crate.

No food.

No water.

And for Heaven's sake, don't stimulate the pee and poop out of your dog with extra attention maybe by asking him "what's wrong?"

I'll tell you what's wrong and how you can fix it!

Your dog perceives that if he poops, something will kill him.

His Self Preservation stops him from pooping.

Let's put it in human terms.

Did you ever take a wrong turn into the bad side of town?

Did you ever walk into a bar and feel the hair stand up on the back of your neck?

Have you ever had an overwhelming I-gotta-get-the-Hello-Dolly-out-of-here feeling?

That's your Self Preservation Drive at work.

Just imagine having that feeling as you are about to take the throne, in the bathroom, in a biker bar, old dirty gas station or any strange, uncomfortable place.

Could you perform?

Probably not.

Your dog is having a similar Self Preservation experience and you need to exchange his natural, evolved reaction for a new conditioned reaction.

After you put Pookie in the crate, wait a few minutes, five or ten tops, and then take him out to the same potty area and the same exact potty spot.

A reasonably short time between trips outside is critical and necessary to establish a pattern, versus a random number of separate, single events.

After three or four times, this will show your dog that nothing bad happens. His brain observes that it's safe and familiar and his self preservation drive turns off.

Click!

Once this association is established, and it could take a while, he feels physically safe to potty in that location.

Do a set of four repetitions and then give his brain a break to process what has just happened. It may take many trips outside, but this is the only solution and it's what will make him do his business.

So, to review our rebounding technique:

You take Pookie out. He doesn't go potty.

You go in and put Pookie in the crate.

Five or ten minutes later you take him out again and repeat until he goes.

Keep in mind, if Pookie doesn't go, he stays in the crate until he does go outside.

Even if he stays in the crate all day or overnight.

If you put him in the crate and he starts doing the potty dance, take him out immediately.

If you want your self preserving dog to go potty outside, *Rebound!*

And a One and a Two

Making your dog go number two on command.

So, what about Number Two?

Good question.

When your dog begins to go number two, twisting himself into that uncomfortable looking, undignified, airplane-landing-position, you quietly, almost subliminally, say, "empty two, empty two, empty two, empty two" as the number two is coming out.

Again, this connects, attaches or marries a cue, a sound, a noise, a grunt (two), to the feeling of pooping and later becomes the "magic" word: the cue, the trigger, the signal that causes your dog to go number two on command.

Saying "empty two" makes sense to your human brain, as we think of poop as number two. It's good for you and your dog.

So, we have successfully had your dog go potty one whole time!

It's a good start, but there is much more to do.

You are establishing conditioned associations, things that happen in connection with one another, and generating a conditioned response.

This will be your routine for at least two weeks, without fail.

The end result is: your dog goes potty, outside, on your command.

Read The Signs

Your dog's natural potty signs.

Many people mistakenly believe their dog should automatically; "ask out" or tell their owner they need to go potty.

When I was a teenager, I thought my dog should walk over to the door, tilt his head to the side, perk his ears, paw a small set of jingle balls and say, "Errrrrrrruhh???" when he wanted to go to potty.

Maybe I was watching too much Scooby Doo and too many Disney movies.

Unless you specifically and deliberately train your dog to give a signal that he needs to go potty, like pawing a bell, as our Cover Dog Anubis does, he will only exhibit the normal potty dance signs.

Here is a list:

* Whining

* Moving

* Scratching

* Standing suddenly or for no apparent reason

* Walking in circles

* Looking at or sniffing his rear end

* Anything suddenly different

Learn to read those signs and take your dog out when you see them.

Preventing Potty Training Accidents

Understanding, anticipating and preventing potty training accidents puts *you* in control, rather than waiting for these unpleasant things to happen.

Let's take a look at the potential causes…

Food Glorious Foooood!!!

Why you should feed your dog only dog food in his dog bowl.

Food affects your dog's stomach and his ability to hold his poop.

And you know how we like him to hold his poop!

If you want your dog to be consistent about going potty outside, you need to be in control of what goes inside your dog.

This includes everything that goes in your dog's stomach: treats, table scraps, trash, roadkill, whatever.

It's all food!

You should only give your dog, dog food, in his dog bowl.

This is the only way you know exactly what he is eating and how much.

So, ditch the treats, table scraps, etc., at least during the potty training process.

I realize that it's very, very hard to discipline yourself and only feed your dog, dog food, when he makes that cute dog face and the, "Mmm Mmmff" sound, right?!

But, feeding your dog treats can cause you to forget the timing of food in and poop out.

Treats may also upset his stomach and cause your dog to lose control of his bowels.

Keep it simple!

Good News!!!

There are lots of non-food ways to love your dog!!!

Here are four suggestions:

1) Train him well and establish a legendary dog & handler relationship on which he can rely and in which he finds comfort.

2) Keep your dog in excellent physical condition (trim, taut, terrific), by having him retrieve a ball, throwing the ball for him about ten times. Do this several times a week. Allow time between sessions for recovery.

3) Feed him the best quality dog food you can afford.

4) Groom your dog in a kind, gentle, loving way. This close, positive, physical contact creates a strong connection between you and your dog that is much better and more powerful than treats.

Feeding Schedule

The truth about how often your dog needs to eat and drink

Many people ask me how often they need to feed and water their dog.

Feeding your dog needs to be logical, nutritional and practical for your life and your dog's life.

You may have heard that you need to:

"feed your dog several times a day"
or
"you have to feed your dog on a schedule"
or
"young dogs need to be fed at night"

All these urban legends are false!

They also make your life needlessly complicated.

When you complicate your life in regard to your dog you may begin to resent him.

Avoid these things, keep it simple and enjoy your dog!

Imagine the first wild Canine who walked out of the darkness and into the light of Man's warm campfire. He brought his primal, evolved characteristics with him; his wants, his needs, his natural urges.

Your evolved canine does best when you treat him with that image in mind.

Let me tell you a brief, misinformed-owner, feeding-caused, potty training accident story:

One night, at about 7pm, I got a rather frantic phone call from the owner of a puppy I had recently trained. The puppy was 5 months old and just a bit fat. He was surely not lacking for food.

The woman that owned this poor dog was having a meltdown. Her very young, recently trained puppy had a whopping two whole accidents in his crate since he came home, and she was losing her mind.

First of all, two accidents for a young puppy in a couple of weeks is great. Most reasonable people would be very happy with that record. So, I pressed to find the problem.

I asked her what the feeding routine was for the dog. That's when she told me the most amazing thing…

The owner told me emphatically and with great authority that Puppy must be fed twice-a-day, or his blood sugar would get dangerously low.

WHAT?!!!

His blood sugar?!!! I know, you're thinking, "That sounds strange to me already!"

Well, she went on to say that Puppy had pooped in his crate in the middle of the night.

Well, there's the problem.

She was loading Puppy up with food and then sticking him in the crate with no way to get that food out.

So, he pooped and peed in the crate.

Go figure.

In an attempt to help her, I explained to the owner that Puppy did not need to be fed twice a day and that, in fact, the second feeding was making him poop in the middle of the night.

She became indignant, on the verge of exploding into a rage and said;

"My vet told me

My dog needs to eat at night

or his blood sugar

will get too low!"

Then she flew up into the air on her broomstick and shot across the sky!

(Ok, I made up the broomstick thing.)

Of course, what she said is illogical and wrong.

Dogs have evolved to live and sustain their bodies quite well, while eating infrequently. They can go days without eating and often do in the wild, so hours are never a problem.

When I told her that only a dog with diabetes would require blood sugar maintenance, she hung up on me.

I mean she hung on me so hard that I'm pretty sure she had to buy a new phone.

I'm pretty sure from the sound of it she smashed that phone down and it was in pieces all over the floor!

This owner let her emotions overpower her sense of reason. She convinced herself that her dog needed to be fed twice a day. It's easy to do, but let your logic be your guide.

Here's the bottom line.

Your dog is an evolved creature that can survive many days without food in a crisis.

No matter what urban legends, myths and misconceptions might say. There is no need to rush home to feed your dog, just because it will be an hour or two or three after the regular feeding time.

He'll be fine.

He's a dog.

Provided you are giving him, shelter, access to water, food every day, and appropriate Veterinary Care, your dog needs to fit into your life as it suits you best.

People frequently ask;

"How many times a day should I feed my dog?"

The answer is once-a-day.

A very young puppy, from birth to eleven weeks, is fed much more frequently and will likely pee and poop after each feeding. That doesn't work for potty training.

An older puppy, from 12 weeks to 24 months, or a mature dog should be fed only once-a-day.

Note:

> Some trainers who are conditioning their dogs to an extraordinary level of strength and fitness may feed that dog more frequently as part of this program.

So, to prevent potty training accidents, feed once-a-day, in the morning.

Because each time you put food in, your dog will put poop out.

Make sure to let your dog get all that stuff out, long before bedtime.

Don't put anything else in.

Look at it logically and feed once, in the morning.

Water

How often your dog needs water

Dehydration

And

Don't let your dog drink out of the toilet

Just as we need to remember food in poop out, we also need to realize that the water your dog drinks eventually becomes pee.

Water-in-Pee-out!

Despite passionate, nearly hysterical arguments to the contrary, dogs do not need constant access to food and water!

And if you give your dog constant access to water during the potty training process, he will have accidents and potty training may fail!

Your dog's body and every dog's body can retain water for a very long time. Providing water in the morning and again when you return home from work is enough during the potty training period.

If you allow it, your evolved canine may drink so much water that he cannot contain it. While it may seem kinder and gentler to give your dog free access to water, it is actually risky and can be unhealthy for your dog.

If you're concerned, test the proper hydration of your dog by pulling up the skin over his shoulder blades. It should feel loose and somewhat heavy, like a wet blanket. When you pull that skin up, it should go back down to its normal state quickly.

If the skin stays in a pinched, formed state and does not go back down quickly, your dog is somewhat dehydrated.

But, most dogs are well hydrated and you don't need to worry.

Why do we feel compelled to give our dogs water every time they move?

Why do we want to make them drink when we think they are hot?

Why do we feel our dog needs to drink as much as possible every time he drinks?

Because we have grown up in a culture and in fact, a world where hospitality is expected and admired:

Scene:

An American home in the suburbs,
guests arrive at the front door and Action!!!

"Hello John, so nice to see you here at our beautiful home.

May I get you something to drink?"

"Coffee?"

"No thank you."

"Iced Tea?"

"Thank you, no."

"Milk, Orange Juice, Root Beer?"

"No thank you, I'm fine."

"Sprite, 7 UP, Coke, Pepsi, Moonshine?"

"No, I really don't want anything, thank you."

"Ovaltine?"

"NOTHING!!!"

We have grown up with the idea that we should provide food and drink for husbands, wives, children, guests and any other people or animals who find their way to our home.

For people, this is ok and demonstrates good manners.

For dogs, not ok, will cause potty training accidents and makes no evolved sense.

Dogs evolved for millions of years to survive in less than ideal conditions, often with very limited access to water. They did not have a water dish filled and ready for them to drink out there in the wilderness, or a stream near their den, or a water fountain coming out of the rocks. And they survived and evolved just fine.

Dogs are fully capable of drinking a sufficient amount of water to maintain optimal health, two or three times a day maximum. Animal control regulations across the country reflect this fact.

In order to help your dog hold his pee through the night, do not allow him to drink at least three hours or longer before you go to bed.

And, please, make sure your dog is not drinking out of your toilet!

We know there are probably lots of bad bacteria in our toilets.

We also use chemical cleaning products in our toilets that may be poisonous to your dog! If you allow him to drink from your toilet, he could be drinking low levels of poisons from those products which could slowly kill him! So, no toilet water for Pookie!!!

Providing and controlling your dog's access to safe, drinkable water is an important and serious matter.

Your dog may find contaminated water in your bird bath, in a bucket, a trash can, a puddle or anywhere else rainwater or other liquids and chemicals can collect. So, find those unconventional water sources and places where chemicals and other liquids can collect and empty them out.

Fresh water, in your dog's water bowl two or three times per day is just right!

A Drinking Problem?

Why dogs may drink too much water and how it can hurt them.

Dogs are evolved animals and not capable of acting in a logical, healthy or safe way, when eating and drinking in our modern world.

So, we have to look out for them!

Domestic dogs will often stand in place over the water bowl and drink so much water that it damages their bladder, bladder sphincter and ability to hold their urine.

By contrast, evolving dogs had to keep moving almost constantly. They would drink at every opportunity and keep drinking until they were compelled to move by a self preservation trigger.

Dogs who did this through evolution, in areas where water was scarce, survived and passed that trait onto our over-drinking, contemporary, domestic dogs.

It was good way-back-in-the-dog-day, but, it's very bad now!

If your dog's bladder is constantly full of urine, and he tries to "hold it", it can weaken his bladder sphincter, the tiny circular muscle that holds the urine in his bladder. Don't let your dog fill up on too much water and strain his bladder sphincter. It can eventually make your dog unable to "hold it" at all.

So, always monitor your dog's water consumption and do not allow or overlook your dog drinking too much water.

Put a lid on it, especially the toilet seat lid.

Let your dog drink just enough water to stay well hydrated.

At the end of your day, I actually mean when your day comes to an end, take your dog out to pee, as close to your going-to-bed-time as possible.

Activity

How activity stimulates your dog to go potty.

You've probably figured out by now that there are a whole lot of things that affect potty training and can cause accidents. Activity is a major factor.

To you and me, when we stand up to go the refrigerator, it's not a big deal and it doesn't make us have to go to the bathroom.

To your young, un-potty trained dog, you getting up and walking out of the room is huge and it does make him gotta-go-right-now!

To you and me, answering the phone is not a big deal.

To your young, un-potty trained dog, huge, gotta-go-right-now!

To you and me, cheering when your team scores a touchdown, not a big deal.

To your un-potty trained dog, gotta-go-right-now!

Any time you are active, a young dog is absolutely stimulated to go potty. The younger the dog, the more overwhelming the activity can be. You may have been completely unaware of this important fact about potty training and it can defeat your efforts.

If you have a young dog and anything happens:

> You stand up from sitting.

> You come home from work.

> You finish watching a movie and stand up.

> You wake up from sleeping.

Take your dog out!

Older dogs can hold it longer, but they are also affected by movement, excitement, sound, scent, and any of these things can cause your puppy or older dog to need to go potty.

So, be vigilant, attentive, and take your dog out any time things get active.

Environment

How the environment affects your dog
and
The story of Memom's afghan

"How can my dog's environment, where he lives and travels, make my dog go potty?" you ask.

The most common way your dog's environment can make him go potty is by your dog or other dogs having gone potty there before.

If your dog, or another dog, has peed or pooped in your house, on your carpet, or on the leg of your chair, that scent can stimulate your dog to pee now, in the future and possibly for the rest of your dog's life.

Keep in mind that your dog's brain, which is about the size of half of an apple and weighs from 60 to 95 grams depending on size and breed, is twenty percent or so dedicated to identifying and responding to odor, by way of the scent receptors and olfactory bulbs. So, if there is even a trace of scent remaining from a dog peeing or pooping, it may stimulate your dog to pee or poop.

Scent from urine or feces can and often does stay in carpet and furniture for years, because bacteria reconstitutes, stimulating marking behavior over and over and over again!

"What do I do?" you ask.

Well, you need to completely eliminate the old scent.

The most effective way I have found is to remove and replace the tainted fabric, wood, or carpet, and pad beneath the carpet, and get rid of the old furniture if possible.

I know this is expensive and a huge pain in the neck that moves ever lower. However, replacing the tainted furniture is always cheaper than having to replace new carpet and furniture because you can't stop the marking on old spots and your dog then marks new spots.

If you can't replace the carpet or remove the old furniture, the most effective way I have found to remove the scent is with enzymatic cleaner. It uses enzymes to eat up the old pee or poop molecules. Any effective enzymatic odor killer will do.

Our sense of smell isn't nearly as good as dogs, but have you ever had:

The Amazing, Eternal Cat-Pee-Smell?!!!

"Just when you thought you had washed out that kitty pee . . . ."

"Just when you thought it was ok to re-use that towel . . . ."

"Just when you thought it was OK to get back under your favorite blanket…"

Dan Dan Dannnnnnnnn . . . .

"It's The Curse of The Kitty Pee!!!"

True Story:

I once had an afghan blanket my Memom crocheted for me.

My sister's evil cat, Wenonah, peed on it!

Her pee was a weapon of Mass Destruction!

Kitty chemical warfare at its' worst!!!

And I really loved that afghan.
I loved it because my Memom made it for me.

So, I carefully, painstakingly washed that blanket.

And Yahooooo!!!

It smelled all better, or so I thought. . . .

"Great, I have my Memom's afghan back!"

I hugged that afghan, wrapped it tight around me, spun and spun with that afghan in a cocoon of Memom love, while happy music played in my head.

Aaaaaaaaannd, the cat pee smell came back.

Wot Wahhhh….

This happened again and again and again, until I finally had to give up Memom's afghan and throw it away!

Tear . . . .

Can you believe it?!

Super Sad....

You may have experienced this yourself, not specifically with my Memom's afghan.

And I'm so sorry for you if you have.

The lesson in all of this is; if you can smell pee, just imagine how strong reconstituting urine or feces scent is to your dog.

You and I have approximately five million scent receptors in our nasal passages.

Anybody know how many your dog has?

Survey Says!.................

Two hundred million!!!

Ding Ding Ding Ding Ding!!!

Wow!!!

The moral of the Memom's afghan story is:

It's hard to get rid of reconstituting urine and your dog can smell the tiniest amount.

The World Around Pookie

How outside forces can and do cause potty training accidents.

When you've done everything right, you know your dog is healthy, and still there are potty training problems, it may be *The World Around Pookie,* that you can't control.

When outside factors affect your dog, he may pee or poop inside your house.

So, let's look at the science behind those factors.

When you're away from home and your dog is loose in the house, the world around Pookie is really cookin'. That can cause your dog to go potty in your house and you won't know why.

You may think you did something or did not do something when, in fact, the world around Pookie is the culprit.

You may think he is being a bad dog, when he just can't help but react to those outside forces.

If, during the potty training process, he looks out the window and sees movement, Pookie may pee or poop in your house.

Stimulation = potty.

If he hears sounds outside, he may pee or poop in your house.

Stimulation = potty.

If the scent or smell of another dog, or person drifts into your house, straight through your walls and windows, your dog may pee or poop in your house.

Stimulation = potty.

> If a big truck goes down the street.
>
> If your doorbell rings.
>
> If, If, If, …

You get the idea.

You may be saying, "Well, what am I supposed to do, live in a library or monastery, where there's no sound or activity?!"

No.

But, you do need to get your dog potty trained and get him accustomed to major stimulation, a little at a time, while keeping him in his crate.

Eventually, intense stimulation will not cause him to go potty. He won't be affected by that stimulation, in that way, anymore.

Eventually, the sights, sounds and smells around your house will become familiar and he will stop reacting to them.

So, when you're away from home, until your dog has long since been

rock-solid-never-goes-in-the-house-can-hold-it-no-matter-what-happens-potty trained,

keep your dog in-the-crate.

As you read earlier, dogs perceive themselves to be safe in their crate, just as they did millions of years ago in their den and are much less inclined to go potty there.

If they do have an accident, at least it's not on your floor or carpet.

So, use the crate!

Let's Be Practical

Equipped with all this information, you may expect that everything will go perfectly.

It may and it may not.

Keep in mind, Pookie is a dog, you are only human, and perfection is rare.

So, let's be practical, stay the course and you will get where you want to be.

The Traveling Potty Show

What to do when you travel

And

What you see versus what your dog sees

Most of us travel from time to time and sometimes we take our dogs with us.

They still need to go potty and you need to know how to make that happen, on the road!

It might go something like this . . .

You've gotten your dog potty trained at home, and yet when you go on a road trip he has an accident at your parents' house.

I thought my precious little Pookie was potty trained!

Well, again, this is your dog, and dogs perceive things differently from humans.

So, when he goes to your parents' house, while you perceive their house as safe, it is simply unfamiliar to your dog.

Here's how dog and human perception differs:

You look up at the sky and see sky.

Your dog looks up and sees muted colors, and up.

Dogs are color blind and see very limited yellows and blues.

You look up at the ceiling and see ceiling.

Your dog looks up and sees muted colors and up.

He cannot distinguish between ceiling and sky, floor and grass.

We imagine that he can, and expect more than is realistic as a result.

Dogs don't see inside and outside.

It's all outside to your dog.

The point is, your dog and all dogs can only see things in two categories:

Familiar and unfamiliar.

Most of the time, after potty training, a normal dog will not go potty in a familiar area where he spends time with his group, sleeps and eats. There are some exceptions, but they are rare. Therefore, you need to establish for your dog that inside your house and each new area where your dog will spend time, eat and sleep, is familiar and a non-potty area.

Well, how do I do that?

When you arrive at the new location use the crate and rebound the dog until the potty training association with outside is set in the dog's brain.

Outside-empty-empty-yadda, yadda, yadda. Inside-crate.

If you are on the road and you do not have a crate, keep your dog on a leash and rebound the dog until he goes.

If your travel plans make this impossible, don't take the dog!

Be practical!!!

Once potty training is proving to be reliable, your dog goes potty outside and doesn't go potty inside, you can allow more freedom in the "new" house.

But, don't go crazy.

Take it slow and get it right.

POTTY TRAINING MYSTERIES

Cue Scaaaaaaarrrry Music…

You may be experiencing *abnormal* potty problems.

Let's cover some of them.

Spite Pee

Your dog doesn't pee out of spite

But

He may have a urinary tract infection

And

The story of Sparky

Sometimes, people convince themselves that their poop-eating, tail-chasing, fallin'-for-the-fake-ball-throw, not-recognizing-himself-in-the-mirror canine, is peeing in their house out of spite.

Could your canine, with a brain smaller than half an apple be capable of:

"a malicious, usually small-minded desire to harm or humiliate somebody"?

(Websters definition of spite.)

Certainly not.

But, check out this story….

Sparky was a Border Collie mix and his owner, Shirley, told me in a heavy Southern Accent she was convinced that,

"Sparky peed on the carpet 'cause he was may-id at me for leavin' him home alone ah-gay-en!"

"Are you serious?" I said.

Dogs don't get angry because they don't have human emotions.

They have their own canine reactions and they are absolutely wonderful, but, they are not human!

Back to our story....

"Come on!" I said to Shirley,

"It's a dawg!"

"He eats his own poop, chases his tail, barks at that dog in the mirror (him).

"It's a dog, Shirley!"

Dogs don't get angry.

They don't do things out of spite.

Rather, they only do what their brain tells their body to do, in reaction to their body or their environment.

Well, of course, Sparky was sick. He had a urinary tract infection. This is actually common in male dogs. We got Sparky treated with antibiotics. The urinary tract infection cleared up and presto-chango he was potty trained again.

Sparky's "spite" was cured, right along with his urinary tract infection, strangely enough.

Keep this story in mind as you evaluate your dog.

The Real Deal

Why your dog pees on your stuff.

So, why would my dog pee on my stuff . . . ?

Your dog may have peed on your bed, your couch or something of yours, you got really mad and you wondered what in the world was going on.

This section will explain that seemingly bizarre behavior, and replace hot-headed supposition with rock-solid science.

Sick dogs or dogs with an overflowing bladder will often go to a place where the owner's scent is strong, when they are feeling the need to pee.

They may go to:

> The bed.

> The couch.

> Or come to the owner and suddenly empty their bladder.

> And if your dog does this you should feel good about it!

You might be thinking,

> "That just sounds weird!"

> Well, let me explain.

Your dog associates peeing safely with you, his owner. Of course!

You take him out to go potty and he doesn't get hurt.

You tell him, "Good Boy!"

Thus, your dog wants to get to you, or your scent, when he feels the urge to pee.

> Wanna know why?

> Your scent and you are the same thing to your dog!

Your dog feels the need to hold his pee, an evolved behavior that saves an animal from detection by predators, until his doggie brain says he is safe.

You equal safety.

You equal comfort.

Your scent equals you.

Even if you just finished sweating to the oldies, ate fresh garlic and smell like a bag of old gym socks, to your dog, your scent equals safety and comfort, and when he reaches your scent, he pees.

He perceives the sock, the shoe, the underwear, the pillow, the mattress or the couch marked with your scent to be you . . .

Most owners don't realize what is happening, get it wrong and punish the dog.

He absolutely can't process why you are angry when he pees near you or on your stuff.

Sometimes dogs even pee on their owners!

Now, wouldn't you feel terrible if you yelled at your dog or worse, because he wanted to be safe when peeing?

Imagine, for a moment, that your dog could talk and said to you,

"I was feeling really sick and self-preserving and I thought I saw you where your sock was. I thought I was with you and I was finally safe, so I peed."

(Man, that even gets to me…)

Think about it!

Reduce-Reuse-Recycle

Why your dog eats his poop

And

How you may be able to stop it.

People often tell me, "My dog eats his own poop!"

AHHHHHHHHHHHHHHHHHHHHHHHHHH!!!!!!!!!!!!!!!!!!!!!!!!!!!!!!!!!!!!! !!!!!!!

Why in the world do dogs do this?

Well, your dog is not driven by the climate change worry sweeping our planet and trying to reduce his poopy footprint.

Your dog has not signed on to the Canine Anal Consumption Agreement – otherwise known as C.A.C.A.

It's much more primal and self-serving.

Yes, sports fans, it's our old friend Self Preservation making yet another appearance here on today's show.

To review: dogs throughout evolution engaged in random behaviors that resulted in their survival. Those dogs passed their genes and evolved behaviors on to today's dogs, and to your dog.

Specifically, if a dog way back in the early days of evolution ate his own poop, that dog was less likely to be detected, seen or smelled by a predator.

Thus, he lived to poop another day.

Even if it took two or three times. EeeYuuuuukkk!!!

So, your dog today eats his own poop.

Can we fix it?

Mmmmmaybe…

There are products on the market that attempt to discourage dogs from eating their own poop by making it taste bad, and they work, sometimes.

80

One of the best solutions is to potty your dog on the leash and simply move him away from the poop as soon as he stops pooping.

If your dog moves toward the poop, execute a leash correction.

And always be sure to Scoop the poop every time before the next potty break.

At least now you have an understanding of this disgusting habit.

Happy Pee

Why your dog pees when you come home

Frankenstein

And

How to fix Happy Pee.

You come home from a long day at work, open your door and your man's best friend pees all over your shiny, expensive dress shoes.

"Whyyyyyyyyyyyy?"you say, as you stand there looking at the pee on your high dollar kicks.

The answer this time is . . . . Submission!!!

Some dogs have an excessive submission response when this giant, overwhelmingly dominant animal, you, moves in and towers over them.

You imagine you are in a slow-motion romantic scene from a movie:

>Running toward your beloved dog . . .

>He is bounding toward you . . .

>Through the tall grass with love in his eyes . . .

>And...

>And now for the truth…

Your dog sees it more like a terrifying scene from a Frankenstein movie:

>You are the monster: moaning, groaning and grunting in a language he doesn't understand, moving awkwardly, ominously toward him and he can't get awayyyyy!!!

>He is submitting as far as he possibly can to you, but you crouch ever closer, grunting,

>"Eee wee, bee bee, lee bee shee boo!"

At least that's what he hears. And when he can't escape this grunting, squeaking giant, he pees all over the giant's shoes.

Makes sense when you see it from a dog's eye view, doesn't it? Especially when you realize that submissive pee kept evolving dogs from being killed.

Can this be fixed? Sometimes...

Some dogs will eventually develop the association that there is no dominance connected to your arrival, and stop peeing.

Some dogs will be selectively submissive and pee when certain people approach, and some will do it when anyone approaches.

What can I do? . . . . Good question.

It would be wise to keep the submissive pee-er in his crate while you are gone and let your dog out to go potty after he has adjusted to your presence. He may submissive pee in the crate a tiny bit, but, this is better.

When you arrive, make this event as calm and boring as possible.

Stay away from the crate.

Ignore your dog at first.

Don't talk to him.

Don't look directly at your dog.

Once he is calm, bring him out of the crate.

I can hear some of you out there saying,

"I'm not gonna have to keep my dog in the crate forever, am I?!

And for your information, Mr. Dog Trainer, I am not gonna ignore my dog and have to be quiet in my own house!"

Well, it's not forever. It's just during the training phase.

And, you only have to be quiet arriving home until your dog is potty trained.

If you don't do it this way you may have a dog who pees and poops in your house his entire life or until you get rid of the dog.

So, a couple of weeks isn't so bad. Is it?

You may be intending to greet your dog in the very best spirit of kindness, but remember he's a dog!

Dogs don't get your intentions, understand what you are saying and can't read your mind. They can only react to what they experience, in their evolved canine perception.

The moral of this story is: keep your dog in the crate, relieve as much dominance as possible and you may eliminate the elimination.

"X" Marks The Spot

Why dogs mark

How to stop it

And

How to choose a dog without this inherited behavior.

Through evolution, canines who marked their territory and attacked those who entered their marked territory, survived at a much higher rate than those who did not. Then they made more canines just like them.

The resulting evolved marking sequence is as follows:

Your dog moves to the edges of his territory, his Dominance Drive is activated; your dog marks.

Or, your dog smells foreign pee, his Dominance Drive is activated; your dog marks.

Can you stop it?

Sometimes.

Some dogs will stop marking if there is a negative association with marking.

I have found correcting a marking dog just as he begins to mark to be most effective.

But, it does not always work.

Many people believe that castrating a male dog will absolutely stop marking.

This is false.

The canine brain can compel a castrated dog to mark as well.

Potty training the dog in the very beginning can fix the tendency to mark by directly associating marking with correction.

Dog begins to raise his leg, you say Aus (the German word for out) and tug the leash sharply.

Watch for him to repeat the attempt, and when he starts to raise his leg, tug the leash sharply again.

You will need to set up this scenario and induce the behavior, in order to be in position to correct the dog and create a negative association with marking.

Repeat the process in sets of four repetitions.

Do not allow the dog to have the opportunity to mark without the correction.

This means you will have to crate the dog during the training process.

Marking behavior is very unpleasant and it is usually inherited from the male parent. Check to see if your dog's father marks before you buy your puppy.

In my experience, small dogs mark much more often than large breed dogs.

Selecting the right dog with the right behavioral traits is super important as this dog will likely be with you for many years!

So, ask if the father of your prospective puppy, or an older dog you are considering marks.

If the answer is yes, move on.

It can save you twelve or more years of difficult dogness.

The Big Picture

An overview of what you have done and learned.

Let's review.

You got your dog out, he went potty, you matched the word empty to the feeling, quietly, and you got your dog back in.

Then you put him in the crate.

You've learned how to watch for the potty signs in the crate and when your dog is out of the crate, on the leash.

We know it's you that makes this work.

You know to keep your dog on the leash or in the crate.

You know how to prevent potty training accidents.

You know that food, water, activity and your dog's environment, affect your dog's potty training.

You know the World Around Pookie can cause all sorts of problems with potty training, and that makes the crate even more important.

You know that accidents happen and how to fix them with The Rebound.

You know you have to take your potty training show On The Road, if you expect potty training to travel well.

You know your dog sees things differently from you, i.e. the ceiling, the sky, inside, outside, and you have to train your dog to have the associations you want in the areas you choose.

You know dogs sometimes, a lot of times, eat their own poop and as strange as it seems, it's normal to their evolved brain.

You know that some dogs pee when they perceive someone or something to be overwhelmingly dominant, even when that someone is you and you are simply saying hello.

You know that some dogs mark and it's pretty difficult to stop.

IN CONCLUSION

The most important thing you can do is read this book several times, from beginning to end, review the material once or twice and refer to it when you have a question or a moment of doubt.

Do this and you will successfully potty train your dog!

Write us at dogandman.co@gmail.com and tell your Dog and Man story.

You may even see it in our next book.

Good luck and let the potty training begin!!!